ChiWOWhua!

Chi WOW hua!

Undersized, Underfoot & Over the Top

WILLOW CREEK PRESS

Published by Willow Creek Press
P.O. Box 147, Minocqua, Wisconsin 54548

For information on other Willow Creek Press titles,
call 1-800-850-9453

Photo Credits: p2 © John Daniels/ardea.com; p5 © Chris Luneski; p6 © Mark McQueen/Kimball Stock; p8 © Chia Wen/Kimball Stock; p11 © Lucy Snowe/SuperStock; p12 © Lucy Snowe/SuperStock; p15 © Ron Kimball/Kimball Stock; p16 © Johan de Meester/ardea.com; p20 © J. M. Labat/ardea.com; p23 © Mark McQueen/Kimball Stock; p24 © age fotostock/SuperStock; p27 © Sharon Eide/Elizabeth Flynn; p28 © Ron Kimball/Kimball Stock; p31 © Dale O'Dell/SuperStock; p32 © Norvia Behling; p35 © Jerry Shulman/SuperStock; p36 © Sharon Eide/Elizabeth Flynn; p39 © age fotostock/SuperStock; p40 © age fotostock/SuperStock p43 © Mark McQueen/Kimball Stock; p44 © Biosphoto/Klein J.-L. & Hubert M.-L./Peter Arnold Inc.; p47 © John Daniels/ardea.com; p51 © Lucy Snowe/SuperStock; p52 © Mark McQueen/Kimball Stock; p55 © Klein & Hubert/BIOS/Peter Arnold, Inc.; p56 © Lucy Snowe/SuperStock; p59 © Sharon Eide/Elizabeth Flynn; p60 © Chia Wen/Kimball Stock; p63 © J. M. Labat/ardea.com; p64 © Mark McQueen/Kimball Stock; p67 © J. M. Labat/ardea.com; p68 © Dale O'Dell/SuperStock; p71 © maXx images/SuperStock; p72 © Norvia Behling; p75 © Mark McQueen/Kimball Stock; p79 © SuperStock, Inc./SuperStock; p80 © Mitsuaki Iwago/Minden Pictures; p84 © Jerry Shulman/SuperStock; p87 © Mark McQueen/Kimball Stock; p88 © Nora Scarlett/SuperStock; p91 © Mark McQueen/Kimball Stock; p92 © Sharon Eide/Elizabeth Flynn; p95 © Tara Darling

Printed in Canada

Hello, my name is Tango. Yes, as in "it takes two to..." If you happen to be owned and loved by a Chihuahua, you already understand the whole togetherness thing. Basically, your solo days are over and we are now the center of your universe—and you love it. Admit it.

For those of you not of the previously converted ilk, I hope to convince you that the Chi is by far the finest of companions. After all, as far as we're concerned, the more Chihuahua-holics out there, the better.

We may be diminutive, but our attitude is "look large and in charge." In keeping with our bold personalities, I have taken the liberty (as Chihuahuas are accustomed to doing) of putting this little book together to make sure all of you are aware of some of the not-so-little things that put the WOW in ChiWOWhua!

Chihuahuas were born to go, go, go! There's never an excuse for not taking us along. Afterall, we fit in everywhere.

*A*DVENTURESOME

"If everything seems under control,
you're just not going fast enough."

—*Mario Andretti*

The Chi... poised, dignified and always on our best behavior. RIGHT. Until that annoying friend of yours comes over with her equally annoying Pomeranian.

ARISTOCRATIC

"A true heiress is never mean to anyone— except a girl who steals your boyfriend."

—*Paris Hilton*

Anyone who shares space with a Chi knows that we are all Celebrichis in our own little world. We will happily pose, perform, or otherwise entertain any whim, all for the sake of art of course.

*A*RTSY

"We all live in this world and we all feed off each other. That's part of it. It's great!"

—*Annie Leibovitz*

You might say we are the smallest unit of canine element, the dog in its most irreducible form. Guess that also makes us the building block of the dog universe and a powerhouse of energy.

Atomic

"Whatever is not an energy source, is an energy sink."

—*Marge Piercy*

Chihuahuas are totally portable and excellent space-savers. There's always room for one more. Besides, who needs extra baggage in their lives?

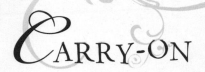

CARRY-ON

"Simplicity is making the journey of this life with just baggage enough."

—*Charles Dudley Warner*

You will find us charming, yes. You will not find us fetching, however. What an unsophisticated way to spend a day at the park!

CHARMING

"All charming people, I fancy, are spoiled.
It is the secret of their attraction."

—*Oscar Wilde*

Okay, guys, so you've figured out that a stroll through the city with a Chihuahua works wonders for attracting the female gender. You'll surely be asked, "Is that a Chihuahua in your pocket…?" Don't let that go to your head. The next line is likely to be, "Ohhhhh, it's so tiny and cute…"

CHICK-MAGNET

"A man who is proud of small things shows that small things are great to him."

—*Madame De Girardin*

And as for you gals out there, no one thinks anything of a girl escorted only by her beloved Chi. Instead of looking dateless and desperate, we make you look chic and independent.

COMPANION

"Her life was okay. Sometimes she wished she were sleeping with the right man instead of with her dog, but she never felt she was sleeping with the wrong dog."

—*Judith Collas*

The point is, we just need to go with you anywhere and everywhere, all the time. And, for the record, occasional phone calls and postcards will not do as substitutes.

COSMOPOLITAN

"I haven't been everywhere, but it's on my list."

—*Susan Sontag*

Dainty schmainty. We may weigh less than a handbag but who do you think dragged your king-sized mattress to the sunny spot in the living room while you were out? Fluffy the kitty? Remember… we go with you everywhere. All the time. Or else.

DAINTY

"I have been uncompromising, peppery, intractable, monomaniacal, tactless, volatile and oft-times disagreeable… I suppose I'm larger than life."

—*Bette Davis*

Given our larger-than-life attitude, Chi's often display behavior and vocal skills in direct opposition to our physical presence.

DARING

"I found my inner bitch and ran with her."

— *Courtney Love*

Chi's have very high standards when it comes to choosing our humans. We are saucy and intense but unfailingly loyal. We only ask that you return the admiration. Seriously, you wouldn't want to be on our bad side.

DEVOTED

"...it takes a strong-minded human
to appreciate a strong-minded dog!"

—*Mary Webber*

"I make enemies deliberately. They are the sauce piquante to my dish of life."

—*Elsa Maxwell*

Though we are people dogs, we do need a little companionship our own size from time to time, so we tend to share our adoration with small plush animals. We are particularly fond of demonstrating our amorous devotion in embarrassing ways in front of your company. Deal with it. Or, better yet, get another Chi for us to play with.

$\mathcal{D}$ISCRIMINATING

"...it can be said without hesitation that two Chihuahuas are just as easy to raise as one."

—Marion Mondshine

We really don't need to remind you that the best things often come in small packages, do we? Consider fine chocolate, rare gems, cell phones, and car keys...

ECONOMIC

"One of the secrets of a happy life is continuous small treats."

—*Iris Murdoch*

Speaking of size, in your big old world, do you have any idea how much time we spend dodging feet, rolling desk chairs, and large derrieres? Crutches are the worst, but we're usually the reason you're on them in the first place.

ENTERPRISING

"If you want to keep your Chi in three dimensions, don't sit or lie down anywhere without first peeking under the cushions and sheets."

—*Brad Rand*

There are a few select members of other breeds that we allow into our elite group of friends. Most of your friends are not included, however.

"If your dog doesn't like someone
you probably shouldn't either."

—*Anon.*

We may not share our time with those we find beneath us (so to speak) but we will always share our fashion sense. Who do you think inspires the Olsen twins?

*F*ASHIONISTA

"Dogs, the foremost snobs in creation, are quick to notice the difference between a well-clad and a disreputable stranger."

—*Albert Payson Terhune*

That's right, we're dauntless, brave, and sassy. Of course, we are also very connected with friends in high places.

FEARLESS

"Bravery never goes out of fashion."

—*William Makepeace Thackeray*

"I hope if dogs ever take over the world and they choose a king, they just don't go by size, because I bet there are some Chihuahuas with some good ideas."

—*Jack Handey*

Once upon a time, this was true: Chi's were once used like little hot water bottles for hands and feet to soothe all your aches and pains. Today we prefer to be known as bed warmers. Or just little hotties.

HAND-WARMER

"All I want is a warm bed and a kind word and unlimited power."

—Ashleigh Brilliant

If you think you're the boss in a household owned by a Chi, well let's just say you must be one taco short of a combination platter. Think again, amigo.

HEAD HONCHO

"I believe in benevolent dictatorship provided I am the dictator."

—*Richard Branson*

That's simply not true! How much work is it to spend every waking moment paying attention to us? Geez, you can do that on the couch.

$\mathscr{H}$IGH-MAINTENANCE

"I just bought a Chihuahua. It's the dog for lazy people. You don't have to walk it. Just hold it out the window and squeeze."

—Anthony Clark

What? Just because we flip in circles, leap a vertical five feet without a running start, bark for no reason, and are highly suspicious of strangers? Did you know that Chi is the Chinese word for the natural energy of the universe? Would you prefer b-o-r-i-n-g?

HIGH-STRUNG

"If you're pretty happy, but you have a little Chihuahua that's always biting you on the ankles, still that's pretty good isn't it? I'm going to go ahead and keep you in the happy category."

—Jack Handey

Chihuahuas must be right in the thick of all that goes on in your life. We're nosy to the extreme. We know you think so; we've read it in your diaries. You ought to be thanking us for screening all those so-called "matches" that pop up all day from the online dating service.

Inquisitive

"On the Internet, nobody knows you're a dog."
—*Peter Steiner*

Cost of new designer underwear: $100. Cost of professional cleaning service to remove stains from carpeting: $250. Your sweet, darling little Chi's face: priceless.

$\mathscr{I}$RRESISTIBLE

"It's kind of fun being the cute, little one.
In fact, I'm finding it hard to grow out of that."

—*Katie Holmes*

For a Chihuahua, the sky's the limit when it comes to exploring bold new horizons with you. We will boldly go... well, where ever.

*J*ET-SETTER

"The cool thing about being famous is traveling. I have always wanted to travel across seas, like to Canada and stuff."

—*Britney Spears*

Okay, so sometimes we can get a little whiney, making mountains out of molehills if the slightest little disturbance disrupts our equilibrium. But, hey, molehills look pretty big from our vantage point.

$\mathcal{M}$ELODRAMATIC

"I know I can be diva-ish sometimes, but I have to be in control. The nature of my life, the nature of what I do, is divadom, it really is."

—*Mariah Carey*

Ah, the paparazzi, they follow us everywhere. Where do you think the expression "SAY CHI'S" comes from?

Notorious

"I never claimed to be famous.
Notorious I have always been."

—Lola Montez

Taking into consideration the hot spots we frequent, Chihuahuas have perfected the art of what happens at the club, stays at the club.

OUTRAGEOUS

"I have Social Disease. I have to go out every
night. If I stay home one night I
start spreading rumors to my dogs."

—Andy Warhol

Sharing your fondness for late night social engagements, we'll certainly hang with you while you catch some extra shut-eye the next morning.

PARTY ANIMAL

"The less I behave like Whistler's mother the night before, the more I look like her the morning after."

—*Tallulah Bankhead*

Your Chi will always be there for you. Rain or shine, we'll be just the lift you need.

$\mathcal{P}$ICK-ME-UP

"When a person is down in the world, an ounce of help is better than a pound of preaching."

—*Edward G. Bulwer-Lytton*

The truth is, we like being small and close to you. Who wants to soar like an eagle? You never hear of a Chi getting sucked into a jet engine.

PINT-SIZED

"Some people see the cup as half empty. Some people see the cup as half full. I see the cup as too large."

—*George Carlin*

Legend has it that Chihuahuas were once involved in certain ceremonies of the Aztecs, like leading the dead through the fearful passages of the underworld. Hmmmmm. You're more likely to find us leading you through the revolving door at Saks these days.

$\mathscr{S}$ACRED

"...No longer worshipped by throngs from afar, it [the Chihuahua] has adjusted quite well to being worshipped by one family at a time."

—D. Caroline Coile

Anything short of idolizing your Chihuahua might not bode well—we have looooong memories that coincide with our looooong life expectancies. Yep, fifteen plus years is a long time to hold a grudge. (How many Zsa Zsa Gabor years is that anyway?)

$\mathscr{S}$ENSITIVE

"Most of us can forgive and forget;
we just don't want the other person
to forget that we forgave."

—*Ivern Ball*

Yes, Chi's are instinctively snappy, chic, handsome, tuned-in, and highly intelligent. "Sharp" is not just a reference to our needlelike tarsal teethers.

$\mathscr{S}$HARP

"Style is primarily a matter of instinct."

—*Bill Blass*

Isn't it nice to know, in this crazy day and age, that you can always count on your Chi for endless affection?

$\mathscr{S}$NUGGLER

"You can't buy love on eBay."

—*Anon.*

While we prefer to bask in the warmth of your lap, on the rare occasion that we are not nestled there or hanging from your hip, you'll find us in the sunniest spot in the house.

$\mathscr{S}$un $\mathscr{W}$orshipper

"If Chihuahuas were people, you'd find them in the hammock on sunny summer days, instead of hiking, canoeing or swimming."

—*Jacqueline O'Neil*

Should you find us shaking like Michael Jackson on his wedding night, please know that this is merely a request for a warmer outfit. If we're out and about, please leave grandma's throw at home. We'd prefer a fine hand-knit sweater.

THIN-SKINNED

"Has a woman who knew she was well-dressed ever caught a cold?"

—*Friedrich Nietzsche*

You can tell your friends all you want about how sweet and calm and well-behaved your Chi is, but in the meantime we'll be piddling on your guest's knock-off Gucci tote bag. Think of this as yet another of our contributions to the fashion industry.

Unpredictable

"When people expect me to go right,
I'll go left. I'm unpredictable."

—*Paula Abdul*

Well, that's just ridiculous isn't it? At least if you're looking for a brute to rip an intruder from limb to limb. If, however, what you mean by "watch dog" refers to a preference of adornments, we would be better known as "jewel-encrusted collar" dogs.

Watch Dog

"Jewelry takes people's minds off your wrinkles."

—Sonja Henie

Certainly you didn't think this might imply
the proper etiquette while leashed, did you?

$\mathcal{W}$ELL-HEELED

"I did not have three thousand pairs of
shoes; I had one thousand and sixty."

—*Imelda Marcos*

Life just wouldn't be the same without
the contagious Chihuahua *joie de vivre*.

*Z*ESTFUL

"Something that would make me remember what joy
felt like. Something miraculous, something magical,
something I couldn't believe existed.
Something like… a Chihuahua?"

—*Mary Beth Crain*

*O*kay, so we admit we take some pleasure in being itty-bitty, cutesy pooches to dress up and carry around. What's the harm in that? Who wouldn't like all that attention? I know a Newfie or two who wish they could walk in our shoes. We hope you also realize that size is really a state of mind. When it comes to character, we are ginormous.

You've probably also figured out that, how shall I put this, we are a little attached when it comes to our people. So, I guess you could say that our relationship is an even two-way street. Well, okay, you're going to have to do the shopping part... but we'll make sure not a day goes by that we don't show you how much we love you.